OUR PLANET EARTH

Caves

by Sara Green

BELLWETHER MEDIA • MINNEAPOLIS, MN

Blastoff! Readers are carefully developed by literacy experts to build reading stamina and move students toward fluency by combining standards-based content with developmentally appropriate text.

Level 1 provides the most support through repetition of high-frequency words, light text, predictable sentence patterns, and strong visual support.

Level 2 offers early readers a bit more challenge through varied sentences, increased text load, and text-supportive special features.

Level 3 advances early-fluent readers toward fluency through increased text load, less reliance on photos, advancing concepts, longer sentences, and more complex special features.

★ **Blastoff! Universe**

Reading Level

Grade **K**

Grades **1–3**

Grade **4**

This edition first published in 2022 by Bellwether Media, Inc.

No part of this publication may be reproduced in whole or in part without written permission of the publisher. For information regarding permission, write to Bellwether Media, Inc., Attention: Permissions Department, 6012 Blue Circle Drive, Minnetonka, MN 55343.

Library of Congress Cataloging-in-Publication Data

Names: Green, Sara, 1964- author.
Title: Caves / Sara Green.
Description: Minneapolis, MN : Bellwether Media, 2022. | Series: Blastoff! readers. Our planet Earth | Includes bibliographical references and index. | Audience: Ages 5-8 | Audience: Grades 2-3 |
Summary: "Simple text and full-color photography introduce beginning readers to caves. Developed by literacy experts for students in kindergarten through third grade"-- Provided by publisher.
Identifiers: LCCN 2021011383 (print) | LCCN 2021011384 (ebook) | ISBN 9781644875209 (library binding) | ISBN 9781648344886 (paperback) | ISBN 9781648344282 (ebook)
Subjects: LCSH: Caves--Juvenile literature.
Classification: LCC GB601.2 .G743 2022 (print) | LCC GB601.2 (ebook) | DDC 551.44/7--dc23
LC record available at https://lccn.loc.gov/2021011383
LC ebook record available at https://lccn.loc.gov/2021011384

Editor: Rebecca Sabelko   Designer: Jeffrey Kollock

Printed in the United States of America, North Mankato, MN.

Table of Contents

What Are Caves?

Caves are natural openings in the earth. Most are underground.

Some caves are small.
Others are as large as whole
cities! They form over thousands,
or even millions, of years.

There are many types of caves. Solution caves are the most common. They often form underground in rock or **minerals**.

Mammoth Cave

Famous For

- World's longest cave

- More than 400 miles (644 kilometers) of passageways

solution cave

Temperature

- Around 54 degrees Fahrenheit (12 degrees Celsius)

Mammoth Cave National Park, Kentucky, United States

Rainwater moves into cracks.
It breaks down the rock.
Over time, open spaces form.

stalactite

column →

stalagmite →

Solution caves have **stalactites** and **stalagmites**. Stalactites hang from ceilings. Stalagmites rise from floors.

Stalactite and Stalagmite Formation

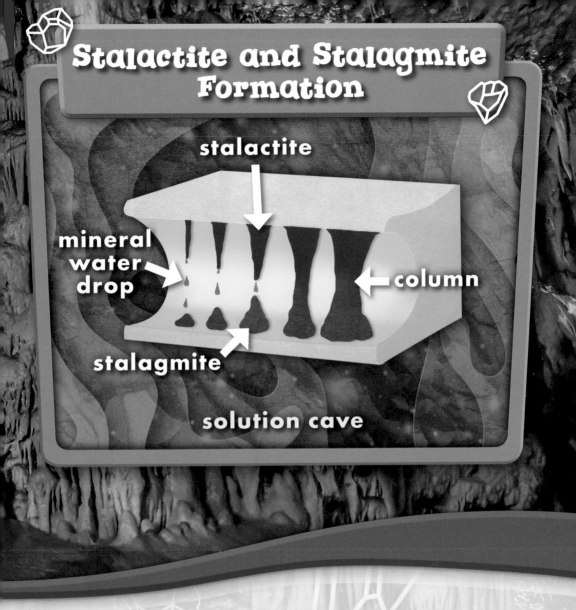

stalactite

mineral water drop

column

stalagmite

solution cave

Both are formed when the minerals in water drops harden over time. Over many years, they may meet and make **columns**!

Caves called **lava** tubes form on **volcanoes**. Hot lava flows under hard surfaces to create tunnels.

Krubera (Voronya) Cave

Famous For

- **One of the world's deepest caves**

- **Around 7,188 feet (2,191 meters) deep**

Temperature

- **Between 36 and 46 degrees Fahrenheit (2 to 7.5 degrees Celsius)**

solution cave

Europe

Krubera (Voronya) Cave, Georgia

glacier cave

lava tube

Melting ice makes **glacier** caves. Warmer water flows through cracks to make large openings.

barn owls

little brown bats

Many animals make their homes in caves. They often live in total darkness.

Some **insects**, fish, shrimp, and salamanders are blind. Their other senses help them survive in the dark.

Cave Animals

Mexican blind cavefish

olm

tailless whip scorpion

Kentucky cave shrimp

Bears often **hibernate** in caves.
Bats sleep in caves during the day.
Many insects eat bat poop!

hibernating
black bears

fruit bats

Plants grow in cave entrances. Roots grow through ceilings and walls. They provide food and shelter for cave dwellers.

People and Caves

Early humans commonly used caves. They left drawings of their beliefs and activities.

Today, **cavers** explore caves for adventure and science. They make maps of unexplored caves. They study formations, art, and life.

cave art

caver

pollution

Exploring caves can be fun and exciting. However, cavers may mark the walls and cause damage.

Their lights and body heat affect cave life. **Pollution** also harms cave **habitats**.

How People Affect Caves

- People cause damage and mark the walls

- Heat and light from cavers disturb cave life

- Pollution harms cave habitats

19

People can help **preserve** caves. Cavers should leave no trace of their visits.

Above ground, people must keep the land, air, and water clean. These practices help protect caves and the animals that depend on them!

Glossary

cavers—people who explore caves

columns—cave formations that occur when stalactites and stalagmites come together

glacier—a massive sheet of ice that covers a large area of land

habitats—lands with certain types of plants, animals, and weather

hibernate—to spend winter sleeping or resting

insects—small animals with six legs and hard outer bodies; an insect's body is divided into three parts.

lava—hot liquid rock that flows out of the earth

minerals—solid materials that are formed naturally in the earth

pollution—anything that makes the earth dirty and unhealthy

preserve—to keep safe from harm

stalactites—cave formations that hang down from the ceiling

stalagmites—cave formations that grow up from the floor

volcanoes—holes in the earth; when a volcano erupts, hot ash, gas, or melted rock called lava shoots out.

To Learn More

AT THE LIBRARY

Amstutz, Lisa J. *Caves*. North Mankato, Minn.:
Capstone, 2020.

London, Martha. *Bats*. Mendota Heights, Minn.:
Focus Readers, 2020.

London, Martha. *Cave of Crystals*. Minneapolis, Minn.:
Abdo Publishing, 2021.

ON THE WEB

FACTSURFER

Factsurfer.com gives you
a safe, fun way to find
more information.

1. Go to www.factsurfer.com.

2. Enter "caves" into the search box
   and click Q.

3. Select your book cover to see a list
   of related content.

Index

The images in this book are reproduced through the courtesy of: Alexandra Lande, front cover; MarcelClemens, p. 3; TayHamPhotography, pp. 4-5; Suthikait Teerawattanaphan, p. 5; Clint Farlinger/ Alamy, p. 6; LKHentry, pp. 6-7; weniliou, pp. 8-9; Yuri Kasyan/ Wikimedia Commons, p. 10; Jane Rix, pp. 10-11; Photo Image, p. 11 (lava tube); Boris Mrdja, p. 12 (owls); Martin Janca, p. 12 (bats); HamsterMan, p. 13 (fish); lucacavallari, p. 13 (olm); Salparadis, p. 13 (scorpion); Michael Durham/ Superstock, p. 13 (shrimp); MilletStudio, pp. 14-15; All Canada Photos/ Alamy, p. 14; imageBROKER/ Alamy, p. 15; acongar, p. 16; Misbachul Munir, pp. 16-17; Tatiana Kkovaleva, pp. 18-19; Richard Bradford, p. 18; GoranE, pp. 20-21; Albert Russ, p. 23.

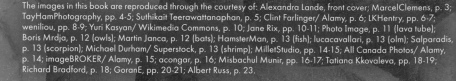